Cocktail and Beverage Making

Water, water everywhere,
And all the boards did shrin
Water, water, everywhere,
Nor any drop to drink!

As Samuel Taylor Coleridge's *Rime of the Ancient Mariner* (1798) warns us; water is everywhere - but drinks for human consumption are an entirely different matter! A drink, or beverage, is a kind of liquid which is specifically prepared for human consumption. There are many types of drinks. They can be divided into various groups such as plain water, alcohol, non-alcoholic drinks, soft drinks (carbonated drinks), fruit or vegetable juices and hot drinks, such as hot chocolate. In addition to fulfilling a basic need, drinks form an important part of the culture of human society. Cocktail mixing and hot beverages (specifically coffee) are the only two sub genres to have really taken the publics imagination however, but today they have evolved into a highly specific and skilled craft form.

A cocktail is a beer or an alcoholic mixed drink that contains three or more ingredients—at least one of the ingredients must be a spirit, one sweet/sugary and one sour/bitter. This is the traditional definition of a cocktail, however today, the term will commonly be used for almost any mixed alcoholic drink, including mixers, mixed shots, etc. The origin of the word 'cocktail' is heavily disputed. The first recorded use of the word *cocktail* is found in *The Morning Post and Gazetteer in London, England* on March 20, 1798:

> 'Mr. Pitt, two petit vers of "L'huile de Venus".
> Ditto, one of "perfeit amour".
> Ditto, 'cock-tail' (vulgarly called ginger).'

The first recorded use of the word *cocktail* in the United States is said to be in *The Farmer's Cabinet* on April 28, 1803, however the *Oxford English dictionary* lists the word as originating in the United States. Regardless of this controversy, the first publication of a bartenders' guide, which included cocktail recipes was in 1862 — *How to Mix Drinks; or, The Bon Vivant's Companion*, by 'Professor' Jerry Thomas. In addition to listings of recipes for Punches, Sours, Slings, Cobblers, Shrubs, Toddies, Flips, and a variety of other types of mixed drinks, were ten recipes for drinks referred to as 'Cocktails.' A key ingredient which differentiated 'cocktails' from other drinks in this compendium was the use of bitters as an ingredient.

HANEY'S

STEWARD & BARKEEPER'S

MANUAL:

A COMPLETE AND PRACTICAL GUIDE

FOR PREPARING ALL KINDS OF

PLAIN AND FANCY MIXED DRINKS

AND

POPULAR BEVERAGES.

BEING THE

MOST APPROVED FORMULAS KNOWN IN THE PROFESSION,

DESIGNED FOR

HOTELS, STEAMERS, CLUB HOUSES, &c., &c.

TO WHICH IS APPENDED RECIPES FOR

Liqueurs, Cordials, Bitters, Syrups,

etc., etc.

British Library Cataloguing-in-Publication Data
A catalogue record for this book is available from the
British Library

During Prohibition in the United States (1919–1933), when alcoholic beverages were illegal, cocktails were still consumed illegally in establishments known as speakeasies. The quality of liquor available during Prohibition was much worse than previously, and there was a shift away from whiskey towards gin - which did not require ageing, and was therefore easier to produce illicitly. Honey, fruit juices, and other flavourings served to mask the foul taste of the inferior liquors. Sweet cocktails were also easier to drink quickly, an important consideration when the establishment might be raided at any moment. After this period, the popularity of cocktails began to wane, however they experienced a resurgence in 1980, with vodka often substituting the original gin in drinks such as the 'martini'. Traditional cocktails and gin began to make a comeback in the 2000s.

Coffee-making, compared to cocktail making has an incredibly long history. Establishments serving prepared coffee, or other hot beverages have existed for over five hundred years. Various legends involving the introduction of coffee to Istanbul at a 'Kiva Han' in the late fifteenth century circulate in culinary tradition, but with no documentation. However, Coffeehouses in Mecca soon became a concern, as they became places for political gatherings. Some Imams consequently banned them, and the drink, for Muslims between 1512 and 1524. In 1530 the first coffee house was opened in Damascus. Soon after, coffee houses became part of the Ottoman Culture, spreading rapidly to all regions of the Ottoman Empire. In the seventeenth century, coffee appeared for the first time in Europe outside the Ottoman Empire, and coffeehouses were established quickly, soon becoming immensely popular.

The modern espresso machine was born in Milan in 1945, by Achille Gaggia, and from there, spread across coffeehouses and restaurants across Italy and the rest of Europe and North America in the early 1950s. Interestingly, the term 'barista' originates from the Italian word for 'bartender', thus linking the professions of cocktail and coffee making. Usually, it refers to a coffee-house employee, who prepares coffee drinks, but can often also serve alcoholic and non-alcoholic beverages too. There are now competitions for baristas to showcase their coffee making skills all over the world. Many professional 'cocktail-makers' today prefer to be referred to as a 'mixologist' as opposed to a bartender, specifically differentiating someone who creates innovative as well as historical beverages. We hope that the reader is inspired by this book to create some beverages of their own! Enjoy.

INDEX.

☞ *The Figures in the following Table of Contents refer to the Numbers of the Recipes, which are numbered consecutively, and not the Paging.*

WINES.

CORDIALS.

LIQUEURS.

BITTERS.

AERATED WATERS.

CONCENTRATED FRUIT SYRUPS.

ACIDULATED SUMMER BEVERAGES.

PREFATORY.

THE object of this work is to afford simple as well as popular directions for the production of mixed drinks. Drinking, the world over, but more particularly in America, is a fixed and recognized social custom—a social custom in and by itself. Even that perpendicular drinking, as it is termed, which so abounds among us, where the ceremony is rapidly gone through with, is, with the growth of our population, steadily on the increase. The revenues derived from the bars of many of our hotels and leading restaurants is sufficient to pay all the expenses, leaving the profits from other sources clear and untouched. At very many of our watering places the bars are leased or rented of the proprietors of the hotels at a handsome figure, by persons altogether disconnected with the other departments of the establishment, and a large interest realized on the investment.

Numerous and varied as is the list of our mixed or fancy drinks, as they are sometimes called, we do not despair of incorporating in these pages all, and even more than those common to the United States, so as to enable any person, with a little practice and strict attention to our recipes, to become in a short time thoroughly *au fait* in their production.

In addition to the benefit to be derived from a perusal of our work by those who propose making bar tending a business, the author has borne in mind those whose tastes may incline them to conviviality, and for this purpose incorporated a number of recipes derived from a multiplicity of sources for the concoction of many delicious beverages in quantities suited to the occasion. They are each and all of them reliable recipes, and will be found, on trial, to be in every particular what they appear in print.

At the great Paris exposition, the American bar was one of the novelties and attractions; and cocktails in the morning were in demand among the people of every nationality.

To the extensive formulas for American beverages we have added Cordials, Liqueurs, Bitters, and other recipes which will, we think, add materially to the value of our Manual. While it is not designed to *advocate* or commend their use, and while we would urgently dissuade all from their abuse, to those wanting a practical and reliable guide to the preparation of any of these articles we believe this volume will be found every way satisfactory.

The most unpleasant duties of the bartender are in the morning, when the bottles and decanters, reduced by the draughts of the day and night previous have to be refilled; the tumblers, used just previous to closing, washed; and everything put in order for the day's operations. Behind all well regulated bars, however, those of our larger hotels for instance, a servant is usually detailed for this duty; but in bars where the receipts are more limited it devolves always on the bartender whose duty it is to make his appearance first in the morning.

A system is in use behind all bars, varying with the caprice of those having charge, regulating the positions of the different bottles and decanters, so that the hand may readily lay hold of them when required. A system of this kind, carefully adhered to, prevents the recurrence of mistakes, and economizes much time; each bottle being always found in its place.

A long white apron is almost an indispensable requisite behind a bar; and in summer time a white linen coat presents a tidy appearance, at the same time being comfortable. A pair of old boots or shoes with slits cut in them, or cut away altogether from the insteps and ball of the foot, are quite as easy, and on the whole to be preferred to slippers.

A well ordered bar should be supplied each day with a number of clean, soft towls, hung conveniently on the outside of the bar for the use of customers. A number of glasses occupying trays should be placed at convenient distances, so that visitors may have no trouble in helping themselves to iced water from the pitchers stationed beside them.

There should be no economy of glasses or decanters— enough of every kind for use always being kept on hand—as they lend a particulary handsome appearance to a bar when well arranged behind it.

STEWARD AND BARKEEPER'S
MANUAL.

—⟞⟝—

MIXED DRINKS AND HOW TO MAKE THEM.

—⟞⟝—

1.—PUNCH.

THIS we believe to be the oldest of all made drinks. Of its origin we are unable to give any reliable testimony. How many a blessing spoken over night, and how many an anathema spoken in the morning, have fallen upon the head of the unconscious individual who first brewed this insidious and seductive promoter of conviviality in mankind?

So many are the different methods employed in mixing punch, that no imperative rules can be given even affecting the sweetness or acidity of the mixture, as tastes differ materially in all things. In making hot punch, it is conceded that it is better to put in the liquor before adding the water; and in cold punch *vice versa*. But really we do not see why a distinction should be made between the two. The precise proportion of spirit and water is like the amount of sugar or syrup used, a matter of preference determined by the palate. A successful punch is where all the ingredients are so amalgamated that no single one is more perceptible than another. This is what bon-vivants claim to be the secret of punch-brewing. A system long in vogue is where the lumps of sugar are rubbed upon the rind of the lemon to extract its flavor, thereby causing the vessels that contain the essence to become broken, and the contents absorbed. But this process is laborious, and seldom followed by the best punch mixers, save when a goodly number are to be supplied.

2.—SCOTCH WHISKY PUNCH.

The sugar should first be thoroughly dissolved in the

hottest of water. The whisky ought to be of the finest quality, Islay being generally preferred. If for a large party, cut the lemon peel thin, and steep it in the pure spirits, or rub upon the peel the lumps of sugar before dissolving ; by either of these means the flavor is successfully extracted. In making a punch behind the bar time is not allowed for either of these processes. As we have before remarked, the proportions are so much a matter of taste that it would be presumptuous to lay down any imperative rule.

3.—HOT BRANDY PUNCH.

Use the best Cognac brandy, it being preferable here to all other kinds. White loaf sugar for sweetening, dissolved in boiling water—just enough for the purpose—this to be done first of all, before the spirits are used. Then pour the brandy into the glass, and add the water, with a slice of lemon, and, if desired, a sprinkling of nutmeg.

4—COLD BRANDY PUNCH.

Fill a large bar glass with chopped or shaved ice; two teaspoonfuls of white sugar; add a tablespoonful of raspberry syrup; two wine glasses of brandy; one wine glass of water; one lime; a slice of pine apple; two slices of orange; berries. The whole to be shaken, and drank through a straw, or with the aid of the strainer. For a party of fifteen use $\frac{3}{4}$ gallon of water ; $2\frac{1}{2}$ quarts of brandy; $1\frac{1}{2}$ lbs. of sugar; 2 or 3 oranges cut in slices; 1 sliced pine apple; $\frac{1}{4}$ pint of Jamaica rum ; juice of 4 lemons ; $1\frac{1}{2}$ gills of raspberry or other syrup; ice. Stir well in a large punch-bowl.

5.—HOT RUM PUNCH.

A wine glass of Jamaica rum ; 2 wine glasses of boiling water ; 2 lumps of sugar well dissolved in a wine glass of water. Put this last into the tumbler; add the rum, and afterward the remainder of the water. Drop in a thin skin of lemon.

6.—HOT WHISKY PUNCH.

For this, use ingredients in same proportion as for hot rum punch, and prepare it after the same fashion.

7.—IRISH WHISKY PUNCH.

The same method is applicable here as in the above. If acidity is desired, squeeze some of the juice of the lemon into the glass before the whisky is poured in. The spirits used should always have age, as Irish whisky, when new, is by no means fit to drink.

8.—COLD WHISKY PUNCH.

This is seldom called for at a bar. Properly, it should first be mixed hot, and allowed to cool, giving at least a day to it when made for a large party

9.—GIN PUNCH.

Use a large bar glass filled with shaved ice; 2 table-spoonfuls of white sugar; 1 tablespoonful of raspberry syrup; 1½ wine glasses of gin; 1 wine glass of water; 1 lime cut into halves; 1 slice of orange; 1 piece of pine-apple. Shake this, and if berries are in season, ornament with them. A straw may be used to sip through. There is another recipe for gin punch as follows: ½ pint of gin; 1 gill of maraschino; 2 lemons, the juice of; a piece of the rind; 4 oz. of syrup; 1 quart bottle of Seltzer water; ice.

10.—CLARET PUNCH.

Large bar glass of chopped or shaved ice; 2 tablespoon-fuls of sugar; 1 slice of lemon; 1 slice of orange. This to be shaken and garnished with berries.

11.—CHAMPAGNE PUNCH.

This recipe is for a party of four; or, if the party are to sit, double the ingredients: 1 qt. bottle of wine; ¼ lb. of

sugar, or even more if called for; 1 wine glass of strawberry syrup; a portion of pineapple, sliced; ½ sliced lemon;
1 sliced orange.

12.—SAUTERNE PUNCH.

This is made in precisely same way as claret punch, substituting sauterne for the other wine. Use large bar glass.

13.—SCADEVA PUNCH.

Fill a large bar glass with shaved ice; 1 tablespoonful
of sugar; 1 wine glass of brandy; 2 slices of lemon; a few
drops of vanilla or other extract. Shake them well. This
drink is seldom called for at a bar, and is known only to a
few prominent bar-tenders.

14.—PINEAPPLE PUNCH.

Pineapple punch is made by adding sliced pineapple to
brandy punch. In preparing for a party, put the pineapple and sugar together in a bowl, and let them stand before adding the other ingredients. A large block of ice
should be used, and fruits generously.

15.—MILK PUNCH.

Use a tablespoonful of pulverized sugar; 1½ wine glasses
of spirits; chopped ice, not shaved*; fill with milk, and
stir slowly with spoon. Sometimes the ingredients are
well shaken, and nutmeg sprinkled upon the surface. This
drink is very nourishing and popular for convalescents
among the faculty. Use a large bar glass. Milk punch is
sometimes made with hot milk, no ice being used.

16.—ROMAN PUNCH.

A popular drink among the fair sex. 1 tablespoonful of

---

*As this beverage is drank directly from the tumbler, without the aid of a straw,
chopped ice is preferable to shaven, the latter being apt to insinuate itself next the
teeth

fine white sugar; 1 tablespoonful of raspberry or strawberry syrup; 1½ wine glasses Jamaica rum; 1 slice of
orange; 1 slice of lemon; 1 teaspoonful of port wine. All
this in a bar glass of chopped ice, to be well shaken, and
imbibed through a straw.

17.—JAPANESE PUNCH.

The juice of one lemon; a piece of the rind; 1 tablespoonful of sugar; 1 slice of pineapple; 1½ wine glasses
of brandy; 1 teaspoonful of arrack; some ground cinnamon. Use a large bar glass filled with chopped ice.

18.—ALBANY PUNCH.

Melt a couple of lumps of sugar; add some lemon juice,
and strain into a glass. Add a wine glass and a half of
Santa Croix rum. Moisten the rim of the glass with lemon.

19.—KNICKERBOCKER PUNCH.

This is made of Rhine wine and curaçoa, a wine glass of
the latter to a large bar glass of the former; a teaspoonful
of Madeira wine; two slices of orange; a few raisins; a
dash of syrup and arrack.

20.—RASPBERRY PUNCH.

One and a half teaspoonsful of raspberry vinegar; a few
pieces of lump sugar; boiling water; 1 teaspoonful of noyau;
1 wine glass cognac; 1 wine glass rum. This is chiefly a
home drink, made in larger quantities and bottled.

21.—WESTERN RIVER PUNCH.

Use large bar glass of shaved ice; 1 tablespoonful of
sugar; 1 pony glass brandy; 1 wine glass of port wine;
lemon juice; 2 slices of orange. To be shaken well, and
sipped through straw.

22.—EMERALD ISLE PUNCH.

Two wine glasses Irish whisky ; 1½ teaspoonsful of sugar·
1 slice of lemon ; 2 wine glasses of hot water.

23.—ARMORY PUNCH.

Use large bar glass filled with ice ; 1 tablespoonful of
sugar ; 1 wine glass of brandy ; 1 pony glass of maraschino ; 1 wine glass of Catawba wine.   Shake the mixture
well.

24.—FRUIT PUNCH.

Use large bar glass.   1 table-spoonful of sugar; ·1½
wine glasses of cognac ; 1 wine glass of Jamaica rum ; 1
glass of noyan ; juice of half a lemon ; 2 slices of orange ;
raisins ; berries ; 1 lime.   Shake well.

25.—CONTINENTAL PUNCH.—(For two.)

1 pint bottle of champagne ; 1 wine glass of brandy ; 3
slices of orange ; 1 slice of pineapple.   Put the fruit into
the glasses, pour over them the brandy, then add the champagne which should be taken invariably from the cooler.
This is a superb punch.

26.—BIRD OF FREEDOM PUNCH.

Two lumps of sugar, these to be dissolved in a little
boiling water ; 1¼ tumbler of Monongahela ; 2 tablespoonsful
of New England rum.   Boiling water.

27.—CHICAGO AND BUFFALO PUNCH.

Equal parts of Catawba (sparkling) and Isabella ; 1
wineglass of sauterne ; ¼ wineglass marashino.   Use fruit,
berries and ice.   Mix in large bar glass.

28.—OCEAN PEARL PUNCH.

One bottle of claret; 1 bottle of soda water; ½ pound of ice; 4 tablespoonsful of powdered sugar; 1 teaspoonful of ground cinnamon; 1 liqueur glass of curaçoa. Put these into a bowl and stir until well mixed.

†29.—ANGLER'S PUNCH.

One quart of brandy; one quart of Jamaica rum; four sliced lemons; ¾ pound of white sugar; 1 quart of water; ½ pint of boiling milk. Steep the lemons in the brandy and rum for five or six hours; add the other ingredients, and strain. This punch is popular among pic-nic parties, and among tourists. It serves well to bottle. This recipe is for a party of fifteen.

30.—LIGHT-GUARD PUNCH

Two bottles of champagne; 1 pint of sherry; 1 pint of brandy; 1 pint of white wine; ½ pineapple, sliced; 2 oranges; 3 lemons, the juice of; sugar to sweeten properly; ice. This recipe is for a party of fifteen. The punch is to be mixed in a bowl.

31.—METROPOLITAN PUNCH.

This punch is composed of claret wine, soda water, brandy and sherry. Add to these lemon juice, sugar and cut pineapple. The proportions are to six bottles of claret and six of soda water, use one each of brandy and sherry. This punch improves by being kept for a few weeks after bottling.

32.—ROCKY MOUNTAIN PUNCH.

Four bottles of champagne; 1 pint of Jamaica rum; ½ pint of maraschino; 4 lemons, sliced; sugar. Mix in large punch bowl. Place in centre of bowl a large block of ice, ornamented with loaf sugar, rock candy, sliced oranges and a bunch of white grapes. This recipe is for a party of fifteen.

33.—CANADIAN PUNCH.

One quart of rye whisky; $\frac{1}{2}$ pint of Jamaica rum; $\frac{1}{2}$ pineapple, sliced; 4 lemons, sliced; 2 quarts of water; ice and sugar.

34.—YALE COLLEGE PUNCH.

One quart bottle of brandy; 1 pint bottle of champagne; two bottles of soda water; 4 tablespoonsful of powdered sugar; 2 slices of pineapple, cut up. Use champagne goblet. Six Yale students will get away with the above very cleverly.

35.—BIMBO PUNCH.

Steep in one quart of Cognac brandy six lemons cut in slices, for five or six hours. Remove the lemons. Dissolve a pound of loaf sugar in a quart of hot water, and add this to the brandy. Allow the mixture to cool before bottling, and use as a liqueur.

36.—ARRACK PUNCH.

The substitution of arrack for brandy in the above receipt, is all that is necessary for the production of a delicate and delicious liqueur; but to make more properly arrack punch, use two-thirds rum to that of arrack. Considerable sweeting is required. Use the juice of two lemons, and add six wine glasses of water.

37.—WEST INDIA PUNCH.

Two quart bottles Santa Cruz rum; 1 quart bottle or Jamaica rum; 5 quarts water; 6 lemons, sliced. Sugar at discretion, with some of the syrup of preserved ginger.

38.—MANHATTAN ISLAND PUNCH.

Squeeze the juice of three large Havana oranges on a pound of loaf sugar; pour upon this a quart of boiling water; one half pint of arrack, and a bottle of brandy, heated. Pare the peel very thinly from a third orange, and throw into the mixture; then stir slowly for half an hour. Drink when cold.

39.—RUBY PUNCH.

This is made of three parts green tea to one one each of arrack and port wine; half a tumbler of lemon juice, and a pound of loaf sugar, dissolved first in the tea.

40.—GOTHIC PUNCH.

Two bottles of still Catawba; a small bottle of claret; half a pineapple, or a couple of oranges if preferred; five tablespoonsful of sugar Cool with ice, and add a small bottle of Heidsieck. These proportions will make sufficient for five.

41.—TEA, OR OLD MAID'S PUNCH.

Make enough tea for the party to be supplied; a cup to each person. Have ready a metallic pitcher, well heated before the fire; into this put some brandy, a wine glass for each of those present; Jamaica rum in the same quantity; and enough of lump sugar, with the juice of one lemon. Set fire to this, and pour in the tea; stirring gently, meanwhile, with a ladle.

42.—BARBADOSE PUNCH.

One quart of Jamaica rum; 1 quart of Cognac brandy; 1 pound of loaf sugar; 4 lemons; 3 quarts of boiling water; 1 teaspoonful of nutmeg. To each glass of this mixture add a tablespoonful of guava jelly. This recipe is for a party of fifteen.

43.—APPLE PUNCH.

Place in a China punch bowl alternately, with powdered sugar between each layer, slices of apple and lemon, the core of the apple being removed. Ice these well, and pour over the fruit a bottle of white wine or claret. Fill the glasses from a ladle.

44.—ORANGE PUNCH.

The juice of three or four oranges; the peel of one or two oranges; $\frac{3}{4}$ pound of lump sugar; $3\frac{1}{2}$ pints of boiling water. Infuse for about half an hour; strain; add half a pint of London porter; rum and brandy, pint each. A glass of any of the liqueurs may be added advantageously.

45.—UNITED SERVICE PUNCH.

This is concocted of arrack, say a pint, with the juice of six or eight lemons added to two pints of hot tea, with three quarters of a pound of loaf sugar dissolved in it; having previously rubbed together a portion of the sugar and the peel of the lemons to extract the flavor of the rind.

46.—MOTHER OF PEARL PUNCH.

Two gallons of Brandy; 1 gallon of water; $\frac{1}{2}$ gallon of tea; 1 pint Jamaica rum; $\frac{1}{2}$ pint chartreuse; juice of eight lemons; $1\frac{3}{4}$ pounds of white sugar. Mix, strain, bottle and keep on ice—the longer the better.

47.—ENGLISH MILK PUNCH.

One quart of old Jamaica rum and 2 quarts of French brandy, mixed; 1 quart of milk, with 2 of water added. Pour the spirits into the milk, stirring meanwhile. Add a couple of cups of strong green tea; a few cloves; the rind of three lemons; one pineapple, peeled and sliced. Allow this to stand for an hour; filter and bottle. When used let it be with ice.

48.—ORGEAT PUNCH.

This is composed of equal parts of orgeat syrup and brandy, with the addition of a little lemon juice. Use for the purpose a large bar glass filled with chopped or shaved ice. A few berries adds ornament, and a dash of port wine additional flavor.

49.—CURACOA PUNCH.

Fill a large bar glass with shaved ice; 1 tablespoonful of sugar; 1 wine glass of brandy; ½ wine glass Jamaica rum ; 1 pony glass of curaçoa ; the juice of a lemon. Shake this well, and ornament with a couple of slices of pineapple, and berries if in season.

50.—SHERRY PUNCH.

Two wine glasses sherry; 1 tablespoonful of sugar; orange and lemon, two slices each. Use large glass filled with shaved ice; shake well, and place straw in glass.

51.—LEMON PUNCH.

The juice of four lemons ; the peel of one lemon ; one pound lump sugar; 3½ pints boiling water ; 2 pints rum or brandy ; ½ pint of porter ; 1 liqueur glass of curaçoa. For additional instruction see recipe No. 44.

52.—NECTAR PUNCH.

Throw the peel of ten lemons into a pint of rum; let it tand for a couple of days ; add a pint and a quart of cold water, with two and a half more pints of rum and the juice of the lemons, with a quart and a pint of boiling milk and some grated nutmeg. Allow this to stand for a day, covered. Add a couple of pounds loaf sugar ; strain and bottle for use.

53.—PUNCH A LA ROMAINE.

Beat an egg with the juice of a lemon; add a tablespoonful of syrup; a wine glass of the finest Cognac; one of old
Jamaica; a liqueur glass of maraschino. Use large bar glass
filled with shaved ice

54.—EGG NOG AND FLIP.

Having exhausted the subject of punches, we will now
consider in order the other drinks which are more commonly
in demand at bars than many of those we have given receipts for. Egg Nogs and Flips are now to be treated.
Egg Nog, we believe, is originally an American institution,
popular both at the North and at the South, but more
particularly in the southern states during the holiday season. It is, with milk punch, popular among the faculty
for the encouragement and aid of convalescents.

55.—EGG NOG.

One tablespoonful of fine white sugar; one tablespoonful
of cold water and one egg; one and half wine glasses of
brandy. Let the glass be filled one quarter or half with
broken or shaved ice. After the sugar, egg, water and
spirits are placed in the tumbler, fill up with milk and
shake well. Santa Cruz or Jamaica rum may be used instead of brandy, or brandy and rum combined, allowing one
or the other slightly to predominate. This drink may be
made hot by using boiling milk without the ice.

56.—EGG NOG.—(For a party of twenty.)

Half dozen eggs; 1 quart brandy; $\frac{1}{2}$ pint Santa Cruz
rum; 1 gallon of milk; $\frac{3}{4}$ pounds white sugar. Beat separ-
ately the whites and the yolks of the eggs. Mix all the
ingredients except the whites, which should be beaten until
they have a light frothy appearance, in a punch bowl, then
let the whites float on top.

57.—EGG NOG.

Here is another method, for a party of twenty or there-
about : 18 or 20 eggs, the yellow of; 15 tablespoonfuls of
pulverized sugar; beat these well together, and grate into
this one nutmeg.   Add 1 pint of brandy or Jamaica rum;
3 or 4 glasses of sherry.   Have on hand, and beat into a
froth, the whites of the eggs ; then beat all together, and
add two and a half quarts of rich milk.   This is a pleasant,
mild and nutritious drink.

58.—EGG NOG.

Sherry wine is not unfrequently used as a substitute for
the stronger liquors.   Put into a large tumbler, quarter
full of broken ice, a tablespoonful of white sugar; break an
egg on the rim of the glass and turn in the yolk ; fill it up
with milk; shake well ; grate on top a little nutmeg, and
drink to the health of your family.

59.—EGG FLIP.

Beat up four eggs ; add half a dozen lumps of sugar, and
stir, pouring in boiling water until the pitcher is three
quarters full, then add three tumblers of Cognac, or two of
Cognac and one of Jamaica rum ; or use rum alone if brandy
be not at hand.

60.—EGG FLIP.

This beverage is more commonly made with ale boiled
in a saucepan ; say a pint.   Beat up the white of an egg ;
add a couple of tablespoonfuls of sugar, brown coffee sugar
being as good as any; pour the ale on slowly and keep
stirring.   Pour back and forth from one vessel to another,
continuing this for two or three minutes.   This is sometimes called Ale Flip.

61.—RUM FLIP.

Follow the directions in the above receipt, only keep the

ale separate until time to mix, when pour into the vessel containing the eggs, sugar, &c., a glass of old Jamaica; then take that holding the ale, and continue pouring from pitcher to pitcher.

62.—BRANDY FLIP.

One tablespoonful of sugar ; one wine glass of brandy. Add to this enough of boiling water; stir; throw in a piece of hard, dry toast, or toasted cracker; add nutmeg and spice.

63.—NEGUS SHRUB.

Negus is not unfrequently made of any of the light wines, but usually of port as that is sweeter and more fruity.

64.—PORT WINE NEGUS.

This is very simple, and prepared in the same way as brandy flip, without the toast, substituting port for Cognac. One teaspoonful of sugar ; one wine glass of port wine ; one tumbler third full of hot water ; grate nutmeg on top.

65.—SODA NEGUS

A very pleasant and refreshing drink. Use a pint of port wine ; six or eight lumps of sugar ; a few cloves ; some grated nutmeg or ground cinnamon. Warm this in a saucepan, pour it thence into a jug or pitcher, and turn in a bottle of soda water.

66.—BRANDY SHRUB.

To the juice of half a dozen lemons add the rind of two lemons. Cover this and allow it to stand for a couple of days. Add a quart bottle of sherry and two pounds of loaf sugar. Strain and bottle it.

67.—RUM SHRUB.

Substitute brandy instead of rum in the above receipt. Sometimes orange juice is used instead of lemon. Considerable time should be allowed for this to stand after corking.

68.—CHERRY SHRUB.

This is made of the sour cherry after it has ripened. Put them into a pot, and place this in another of iron, containing water ; hang this over a fire to extract the juice from the fruit; strain and add sugar. When ready for bottling add spirits, either brandy or whisky. Of the latter Monongahela is preferable, a gill to each pint.

69.—CURRANT SHRUB.

Boil the curarnts and add the syrup of a pound of su_gar to a pint of the juice after it has been strained. Add before cooling two gills of spirits to a quart of the shrub.

70.—RASPBERRY SHRUB.

To one quart of raspberry syrup add a third of vinegar; and to every pint of the shrub put a wine glass of brandy.

71.—JULEPS.

Of all the productions of the bar the julep is, without question, the *chef d'œuvre*. It is essentially and originally American, and is made to perfection in the Southern States where it is universally popular. The varieties are numerous ; but the mint julep is deservedly the most celebrated

72.—MINT JULEP.

Fill a large bar glass with thinly shaven ice ; place on top a few sprigs of fresh mint and a tablespoonful of white sugar ; pour in a wine glass and a half of the finest Cognac ; add a few berries and a couple of slices of orange. Shake this well ; dash with port wine or Jamaica rum. Sprinkle some white sugar on top, and if ornamentation is desired add a few more berries and a fresh slice of the orange, with some additional mint in the center. Imbibe through a straw.

73.—BRANDY JULEP.

The brandy julep is made the same as the mint julep, without the mint. It is like the play of Hamlet, with the, prince left out.

74.—GIN JULEP.

The gin julep is made the same as the mint julep, substituting gin for brandy, and omitting the mint.

75.—WHISKY JULEP

The whisky julep is made like the mint julep, omitting all fancy fixings save the mint.

76.—THE COBBLER.

A delicious summer drink is the cobbler, being with some a favorite over the julep. It had its origin in the United States, and is rather simpler in its construction than the mint julep.

77.—SHERRY COBBLER.

Two wine glasses of sherry; one tablespoonful of sugar; two slices of orange Proceed in this way: Fill a large bar glass with broken ice; put the sugar on top of this; pour in the wine; insert the slices of orange in the ice or lay them on top; throw in some berries if in season, and shake all together. Place a straw in the glass.

78.—CATAWBA COBBLER.

One tablespoonful of sugar; two wine glasses of Catawba; two or three slices of orange. Follow the same method as

in making the sherry co bler.   It is not necessary to mea-
sure the wine, but till the tumbler right up from the bottle;
two wine glasses full are about what it will hold with the
ice.   Sip through a straw or glass tube.

79.—CLARET COBBLER.

Use the same method as in the Catawba cobbler; using
claret wine instead.

80.—HOCK COBBLER.

This also is made the same as the Catawba cobbler, substituting hock for the native wine.

81.—SAUTERNE COBBLER.

The same directions are to be followed as in the case of
the Catawba cobbler.

82.—WHISKY COBBLER.

Two wine glasses of whisky; one tablespoonful of sugar;
two slices of orange.   Follow the instructions given with
No. 77.

83.—CHAMPAGNE COBBLER.

One bottle of wine to four persons; one tablespoonful of
sugar for each glass; one slice of orange.   Fill each tumbler one third full with ice, and the balance with wine.

84.—GIN SMASH.

One wine glass gin; two teaspoonfuls of sugar.   A few
drops of water, some broken ice and a couple of sprigs of
mint.   Add a slice of orange and a few berries.

85.—WHISKY SMASH.

One wine glass of whisky; two teaspoonfuls of sugar; a

few drops of water; a lump or so of ice, and a couple of sprigs of mint.

86.—BRANDY SMASH.

One wine glass of brandy; two teaspoonfuls of sugar; half wine glass of water; some broken ice; a couple of sprigs of mint. Add a slice or two of orange, and berries if in season

87.—BRANDY SOUR.

One wine glass of brandy; half wine glass of water; one tablespoonful of sugar; half of a lemon. Squeeze a portion of the juice of the lemon into the tumbler, which should be one quarter full of ice, and rub the lemon on the rim of the glass. Stir with a spoon.

88.—SANTA CRUZ SOUR.

This is a very popular drink in the summer season, and really one of the most palatable and refreshing that comes. It is made in precisely the same way as the above, substituting St. Croix or Santa Cruz rum for brandy.

89.—GIN SOUR.

Follow the same method here as advised in No. 87, using the ingredients in the same proportion, substituting gin for brandy.

90.—BOURBON SOUR

One and a half wine glasses of bourbon whisky; one wine glass of water; one tablespoonful of sugar; half of a lemon. Squeeze into the tumbler a portion of the juice of the lemon, and rub the rim of the glass. Add a slice of fresh lemon to the mixture.

91.—GIN FIX.

One wine glass of gin; half wine glass of water; one tablespoonful of sugar; juice of half a lemon; ice. Stir with a spoon, and add a slice or two of orange, pineapple or berries if in season.

92.—BRANDY FIX.

Use the same ingredients as in the brandy sour, with the addition of fruits and berries. In the manufacture of fixes and sours a small bar glass or ordinary tumbler is employed, and a strainer placed in the glass to drink through. A small piece of the peel of the lemon adds a flavor to both drinks.

93.—BRANDY TODDY.

One wine glass of brandy; half wine glass of water; one teaspoonful of sugar; one small lump of ice. Stir with a spoon. For hot brandy toddy use boiling water.

94.—WHISKY TODDY.

One and a half wine glasses of whisky; one wine glass of water; one teaspoonful of sugar; one small lump of ice. Stir with a spoon.

95.—GIN TODDY.

One wine glass of gin; one wine glass of water; one teaspoonful of sugar; one small lump of ice. Stir with a spoon.

96.—APPLE TODDY.

Two wine glasses of "Apple Jack"; one tablespoonful of white sugar; half of a baked apple. Add boiling water and nutmeg. This drink ought never to be made with a suspicion of weakness. It is only drank in cold weather, and needs to be a little strong to be satisfactory to the epicurean.

97.—GIN SLING.

One wine glass of gin ; one wine glass of water ; one teaspoonful of sugar ; one small piece of ice. Grate nutmeg on top.

98.—BRANDY SLING.

One wine glass of brandy ; one wine glass of water ; one teaspoonful of sugar ; one small piece of ice. Grate nutmeg on top.

99.—WHISKY SLING.

One wine glass of whisky ; one wine glass of water; one teaspoonful of sugar ; one small piece of ice. No nutmeg. Use for each of these a small bar glass ; and if a hot sling is called for, use boiling water in lieu of the ice.

100.—PORT WINE SANGAREE.

Two wine glasses of port wine ; one large teaspoonful of sugar ; some shaved ice. Shake or stir well with a spoon and grate nutmeg on top. Use an ordinary tumbler.

101.—BRANDY SANGAREE

One wine glass of brandy ; half wine glass of water ; one teaspoonful of sugar ; one small lump of ice. Stir with a spoon and dash on some port wine.

102.—GIN SANGAREE.

One wine glass of gin ; half wine glass of water ; one teaspoonful of sugar ; one small lump of ice. Stir with a spoon, and add a dash of port wine.

103.—SHERRY WINE SANGAREE.

Two wine glasses of sherry ; one large teaspoonful of sugar. Fill tumbler one-third full of shaved ice ; grate a little nutmeg. This beverage is very pleasant when made hot. For the foregoing drinks use the small glass.

104.—PORTER SANGAREE.

Sweeten with a teaspoonful of sugar a glass of the malt, and grate nutmeg on top. The sugar may be dissolved first in a little water.

105.—ALE SANGAREE.

This is made the same as porter sangaree. For both use a large half pint glass.

106.—THE COCKTAIL.

The "Cocktail" is of recent origin, but has rapidly risen in favor. It is most frequently called for in the morning and about half an hour before dinner. It is sometimes taken as an appetizer. It is a welcome companion on fishing excursions, and travelers often go provided with it on railroad journeys.

107.— BRANDY COCKTAIL.

Two or three dashes of gum syrup ; one or two dashes of bitters ; one wine glass of brandy ; one small lump of ice ; one small piece of lemon peel. Stir with a spoon.

108.—BRANDY COCKTAIL.

Two or three dashes of syrup ; one or two dashes of bitters ; one wine glass of brandy ; one dash of absinthe. Fill tumbler one-third full of ice. Stir ; strain into a fancy wine glass ; first squeeze a piece of the lemon peel over, then drop it into the cocktail. Moisten the rim of the glass with lemon.

109.—BRANDY COCKTAIL.

Two dashes of bitters; one liqueur glass of Curaçoa ;

one wine glass of brandy ; one small lump of ice; one piece of lemon peel. Stir with a spoon.

110.—BRANDY COCKTAIL.

Three or four dashes of gum syrup ; two dashes of bitters ; one wine glass of brandy ; one dash of absinthe ; fill tumbler one-third full of ice; stir. Moisten the rim of a fancy wine glass with lemon, and dip it in pulverized white sugar ; strain the cocktail into it, and drop in a small piece of lemon peel.

111.—WHISKY COCKTAIL.

Three or four dashes of gum syrup ; two dashes of bitters ; one wine glass of whisky ; one small lump of ice ; one piece of lemon peel. Stir with a spoon. If requested to strain, use a fancy red wine glass. It is a matter of preference with many to drink the cocktail from the glass in which it is made.

112.—GIN COCKTAIL

Two or three dashes of gum syrup ; two dashes of bitters ; one wine glass of gin ; a dash of Curaçoa ; a small piece of lemon peel. Stir with a spoon. A cocktail should never be shaken.

113 —GIN COCKTAIL.

Two or three dashes of gum syrup ; two dashes of bitters ; one wine glass of gin ; a dash of absinthe ; ice. Stir ; moisten the rim of a wine glass with lemon, and strain it into the cocktail. Throw in a piece of lemon peel.

114.—CHAMPAGNE COCKTAIL.

One teaspoonful of sugar ; two dashes of bitters ; one piece of lemon peel. Fill large bar glass one quarter full of broken ice · fill up with wine ; agitate well with a spoon.

One quart bottle of wine will make a little over four large cocktails.

115.—JAPANESE COCKTAIL.

One liqueur glass of Curaçoa or maraschino; half a teaspoonful of bitters; one wine glass of brandy or gin; one or two pieces of lemon peel; one lump of ice. Stir with a spoon.

116.—SODA COCKTAIL.

One teaspoonful of sugar; two dashes of bitters. Fill glass with soda water and stir with spoon. Use large glass.

117.—CALIFORNIA WINE BITTER COCKTAIL.

Two or three dashes of gum syrup; one wine glass of California wine bitters; one lump of ice; one small piece of lemon peel.

118.—VERMUTH COCKTAIL.

One wine glass of vermuth; one very small piece of ice; one small piece of lemon peel. Serve in a thin stemmed wine glass with curved lip.

119.—HOT SPICED RUM.

One tablespoonful of sugar; one and a half wine glasses of Jamaica rum; one teaspoonful of allspice and cloves; one piece of butter. Fill tumbler three quarters full of hot water.

120.—HOT RUM.

This is made without the spice and butter.

121.—SHERRY AND EGG.

One egg; one wine glass of sherry. Use small bar glass.

122.—SHERRY AND BITTERS.

One dash of bitters; one wine glass of sherry.

123.—BRANDY AND SODA.

Set before your customer a large bar glass one third full of broken ice, and let him pour from the bottle as much brandy as he requires. Then fill up with plain soda.

124.—PONY BRANDY.

Fill a pony glass with best sasarac or ambassador brandy.

125.—BRANDY STRAIGHT.

Place in a tumbler a piece of ice, and set it on the bar with the brandy bottle for the thirsty soul to partake of. This is a good square drink for all times.

126.—GIN STRAIGHT.

Serve this in precisely the same way as the brandy, only make no mistake in the bottles.

127.—GIN AND TANSY.

One third tansy to two thirds gin. Serve from decanter into a wine glass

128.—BLACK STRIPE.

Santa Cruz rum; one tablespoonful of molasses. Is made both hot and cold. Grate a little nutmeg on top in either case.

129.—PEACH AND HONEY.

Peach brandy; one tablespoonful of honey. Stir with a spoon.

130.—STONE FENCE

Bourbon whisky ; sweet cider. This is a western drink. Crab apple cider is frequently used in preference to ordinary cider.

131.—RHINE WINE AND SELTZER WATER.

This is a mixture of Rhine wine with the German seltzer. Place a lump of ice in the glass; fill half with Rhine wine and the balance with " carbonic."

132 —ABSINTHE.

Fill a small bar glass one sixth part with absinthe, and drop the water slowly upon it until the tumbler is three quarters full and the mixture assumes an opalline tint. In most well regulated bars a contrivance for mixing absinthe is always at hand. It consists of a glass, in the bottom of which is a small hole through which the water escapes into the one below in which is the absinthe.

133.—BRANDY AND GUM.

Dash a little gum syrup into a glass containing a lump of ice. Hand it to your customer with the brandy bottle. Stir with a spoon when he has helped himself. He will add water to his taste.

134.—HALF AND HALF.

In England this drink is half porter and half ale, in America old and new ale in equal parts. It is usual to ask for English half and half when porter and ale mixed are what is wanted.

135.—TOM AND JERRY.

Beat the whites of a dozen eggs to a froth and the yolks until they are quite thin ; mix the two together, and add a half tumbler of Jamaica rum ; one and a half teaspoonfuls of ground cinnamon ; quarter teaspoonful of cloves ; quarter teaspoonful of allspice.   Sweeten with about five pounds of sugar, and in serving to customers to a teaspoonful of the above add a quarter of a tumbler of spirits, brandy being preferable ; fill up with boiling water, and grate a little nutmeg on the surface.

136.—WHISKY SKIN.

One and a half wine glasses of Scotch or Irish whisky ; one thin piece of lemon peel.   Fill the tumbler half full of boiling water.

137.—FLUTEMAGINLEY.

One small glass of cider ; half bottle of soda water ; one g ass of sherry ; one pony glass of brandy ; one piece of lemon peel ; sugar and nutmeg. Use large bar glass. This is a somewhat singular name conferred upon a refreshing and pleasant beverage not generally known.

138.—BURNT BRANDY.

This drink is sometimes called for at bars during the warm weather to correct a tendency to diarrhœa. The brandy is poured into a saucer, a lump of sugar placed in the center, and the spirit set fire to.

139.—POST CAFE.

This combination of Latin and French words, signifying, literally, after coffee, is applied to certain combinations of cordials, liqueurs and spirits, in very small quantities, usually partaken of after dinner, and sometimes after breakfast. The recipes for these are neither many nor various.   We subjoin a few below.

140.—POST CAFE.

Fill wine glass one third part each with Cognac, Kerschwasser and Curaçoa.   Use small piece of ice.

141.—POST CAFE.

Fill wine glass one third part each with Cognac, Maraschino and Curaçoa. Use small piece of ice.

142.—POST CAFE.

Fill wine glass one fifth part with maraschino; two-fifths Curaçoa; two-fifths Kerschwasser. Use small piece of ice.

143.—POST CAFE.

Fill a small wine glass half with maraschino; one-fourth with chartreuse, and one-fourth brandy. Use small piece of ice.

144.—BISHOP.

This beverage is made either with claret or port wine. The method is this : Roast a number of good, sound oranges till they are of a brownish color; lay them in a tureen or a small punch bowl, and pour over them enough of pounded sugar, say a pound to eight of the oranges, and six glasses of claret. Do this over night. Cover the bowl and let it stand till next day. When ready, set it in a pan of boiling water; press the juice from the oranges and strain it; heat what remains of the claret; add it to the strained. The glasses drank out of should be slightly warmed.

145.—CRIMEAN CUP.

Peel the thin rind of half a lemon and place it in a bowl with a tablespoonful of sugar; macerate well with a ladle; squeeze upon this the juice of a lemon; add half a wine glass of Jamaica; half a wine glass of brandy, one wine glass of maraschino, and half a wine glass of Curaçoa. Stir well with the ladle. Pour in, still continuing the mixing process with the ladle, two bottles of soda water and one of champagne. Half a pound of ice is also necessary.

146.—CARDINAL.

This is made the same as bishop, substituting champagne for port.

147.—BISHOP (PROTESTANT).

This is hardly more than a rum punch. Mix an ordinary punch of St. Croix or Jamaica, and add claret.

148.—ARCHBISHOP.

The same as bishop (144), substituting claret for port.

149.—CLARET CUP.

One bottle of claret; one pint of cold water; one teaspoonful of ground cinnamon and cloves; one lemon, the rind of. Ice well.

150.—MULLED CLARET.

One lemon, the peel of; five or six tablespoonfuls of white loaf sugar, pounded; one glass of sherry wine; one bottle of claret; one bottle of soda water. More sugar if necessary. Heat it, and serve hot with grated nutmeg.

151.—CHAMPAGNE CUP.

Dissolve some sugar in boiling water, with a little lemon peel; only a few lumps of the sugar. Let it stand for a while, and pour in a quart bottle of champagne with a sprig of verbena; a glass of sherry and two tumblers of water. Mix, strain and ice well.

152.—ORANGEADE.

Half an orange; one tablespoonful of sugar; two slices of orange; one tablespoonful of raspberry syrup. Fill the tumbler with shaved ice; add water; shake well and dash with port wine. Ornament with berries. Use large bar glass.

153.—LEMONADE.

One lemon, the juice of; two tablespoonfuls of sugar; two slices of orange; one tablespoonful raspberry syrup. Fill large bar glass with broken ice; add water; shake well and ornament with berries. Many object to a dash of port, preferring the flavor of the lemon by itself, also the syrup. These may be used or not according to the discretion of the person mixing.

154.—ITALIAN LEMONADE.

Pare a dozen lemons; press the juice on the peel, and let it stand through the night; add a pound of loaf sugar, a pint of sherry and a quart and a half of boiling water. Mix these well; add a pint of boiling milk and strain.

155.—GINGER LEMONADE.

Boil six pounds of lump sugar in five gallons of water; take a quarter of a pound ground ginger, boil with the liquors, and pour it upon half a dozen pared lemons. When cold put it in a cask with a tablespoonful of yeast, having sliced the lemons; add half an ounce of isinglass. Close up the cask the next day; it will be ready in a week or so.

156.—LEMON CREAM NECTAR.

One lemon, the juice of; one tablespoonful of sugar. Fill the tumbler with chopped ice; pour in the soda water, as much as the tumbler will hold; stir well and drink while effervescing. Use large bar glass. Other and very refreshing temperance drinks may be made with raspberry, strawberry, currant or orange syrups. Fill a large tumbler with broken ice; add two tablespoonfuls of any one of the syrups, and as much plain soda as the glass will contain. Stir briskly and drink at once.

157--CHERRY WINE.

No. 1.—Cherries, sound and ripe, thirty-five pounds; brown sugar, five pounds; water, sufficient quantity to make eight gallons; best French brandy, one and a half pints. Add yeast, and set aside to ferment.

No. 2.—Cherries, thirty pounds; moist sugar, five pounds; water, sufficient quantity to fill a seven gallon cask; ferment.

158—CURRANT (RED) WINE.

No. 1.—Red currants, ripe and sound, eighty pounds; brown sugar fourteen pounds; water, to make sixteen gallons; French brandy, half gallon; ferment.

No. 2 —Red currants, bruised and pressed, seventy pounds; brown sugar, ten pounds; water, sufficient quantity to fill up a fifteen gallon cask; ferment. This yields a pleasant red wine, rather tart, but keeps well.

159—CURRANT WINE.

White currants, thirty-five pounds; red currants, thirty-five pounds; rain water, to make fifteen gallons; sugar, ten pounds; French brandy, three pints; press; to each gallon of juice add three gallons water; to ten gallons liquor add thirty pounds of sugar, and ferment. When you bung it up, add brandy two pounds to each ten gallons of wine.

160—BLACK CURRANT WINE.

No. 1.—Black currants, eight pounds; brown sugar, fourteen pounds; rain water, to make fifteen gallons; French brandy, half gallon; ferment.

No. 2.—Black currants, twenty pounds; brandy, two pounds; water, twelve or fourteen gallons; yeast, a sufficiency. These fermented for eight days, then bottled and well corked, yield a pleasant, rather vinous, cooling liquor of a purple color, or they may be made into wine like the

common currants ; by the first process the wine is dark pur
ple, rather thick, but good.

161—ELDER WINE.

No 1.—Elderberries, six gallons ; boiling water, four
gallons ; brown sugar, twenty pounds ; cloves, two ounces ;
ginger, bruised, six ounces ; French brandy, one quart.

No. 2.—Juice of the berries, eight gallons ; water, twelve
gallons ; brown sugar, sixty pounds. Dissolve by boiling ;
add yeast and ferment ; then add brandy, four pounds ; and
bung it up for three months. Disagreeable when cold, but
if mulled with allspice and drank warm in winter time, it
forms a useful stimulant.

162—GINGER WINE.

No. 1.—Best Jamaica ginger, half pound ; rain water,
seven gallons ; refined sugar, twenty pounds. Boil these
together for about half an hour ; cool down to 72° Fahr.,
and add fresh lemon peel, half pound ; yeast, a sufficiency.
Set aside for about fourteen days, and having added a quart
of French brandy, fill into bottles.

No. 2.—Bruised ginger, twelve pounds ; water, ten gallons. Boil for half an hour ; add sugar, twenty-eight pounds ;
boil till dissolved, then cool and put the liquor along with
fourteen lemons sliced, and three pounds of brandy ; add a
little yeast and ferment ; bung it up for three months and
then bottle it.

163—GOOSEBERRY WINE.

No. 1.—Brown sugar, seven pounds ; gooseberries, forty
pounds ; rain water, to make ten gallons ; brandy, one
quart ; ferment.

No. 2.—Ripe berries, ten gallons ; water, thirty gallons.
Soak twenty-four hours ; strain ; to each gallon add Lisbon
sugar, two pounds, and ferment.

No. 3.—Bruised berries, eighty pounds ; water, ten gallons.   Soak for a day; strain; to each gallon add loaf sugar, six pounds, and ferment.

164—GRAPE WINE.

Grapes, forty pounds; refined sugar seven pounds; rain water, to make ten gallons; French brandy, one quart.

165—LEMON WINE.

Four lemons, sliced; brown sugar, two pounds; rain water, two gallons; raisins, two pounds; ferment.

166—ORANGE WINE.

No. 1.—Juice of four dozen Seville oranges; fresh peel of oranges; refined sugar, ten pounds; water, five gallons; best French brandy, one pint.

No. 2.—Sugar, twenty-three pounds; water, ten gallons; boil; clarify with the white of six eggs; pour the boiling liquor upon the parings of one hundred oranges, add the strained juice of these oranges, and yeast, six ounces; let it work for three or four days, then strain it into a barrel; bung it up loosely; in a month add four pounds of brandy, and in three months it will be fit to drink.

167—RAISIN WINE.

No. 1.—Malaga raisins, twenty pounds; water, two gallons.   Boil these together and proceed as directed.

No. 2.—Raisins, one hundred pounds; water, sixteen gallons.   Soak for a fortnight, stirring every day; press; put the liquor in a cask with the bung loose till it has done hissing, then add brandy, four pounds, and bung up close; some use little more than half or two-thirds of this quantity of raisins.

Wines may also be made of blackberries and other fruits, upon the same principles.   The above are the methods generally employed, but most persons have peculiar ways of proceeding, which may indeed be varied to infinity, and so as to produce at pleasure a sweet or dry wine ; the sweet not being so thoroughly fermented as the dry. The addition of brandy destroys the proper flavor of the wine, and it is better to omit it entirely (except for elder or port wine, whose flavor is so strong that it cannot well be injured) and to increase the strength by augmenting the quantity of the raisins or sugar. In general, the most of wines ought to be made of raisins, six pounds, or sugar, four pounds to the gallon, allowing for that contained in the fruit.

168.—MIXED FRUIT WINES.

White currants, three sieves ; red gooseberries, two sieves. These should yield of juice, forty pints; to each gallon add water, two gallons ; sugar three and a half pounds ; ferment.

169.—PARSNIP WINE.

May be made by cutting the root into thin slices, boiling them in water, pressing out the liquor and fermenting it; this wine, when made strong, is of a rich and excellent quality and flavor.

170—METHEGLIN.

Honey, one hundred pounds ; boiling water; sufficient quantity to fill a half hogshead or a thirty-two gallon cask ; stir it well for a day or two ; add yeast, and ferment. Some boil the honey in the water for an hour or two, but this hinders its due fermentation.

171—CORDIALS.

Formerly all these were made from the herbs or fruits whose names they bear, and owing to the large amount of labor required in the preparation of them, few but the professed cordial maker ever thought of attempting their manufacture. These last few years have, however, produced a change in this respect. British cordials are now regularly made in the principal establishments of gentlemen who have two or three branch shops. By the following receipts any quantity of cordial can be made in a very short time, without presses, vats, or other apparatus.

172—ANISEED.

Oil of aniseed, quarter ounce ; spirit of wine (60 O. P.), five pints ; cordial syrup, eleven pints. First dissolve the oil in the spirit by shaking both well together in the jar, and then add the syrup, again agitating briskly. Should the mixture be at all cloudy, fine with alum and salts of tartar.

173—CARRAWAY.

English oil of carraway, quarter ounce ; spirit of wine (60 O. P.), three and a half pints ; cordial syrup, thirteen pints. Dissolve the oil in the spirit as above, add the syrup, and if necessary fine with alum and tartar.

174—CLOVES.

English oil of cloves, quarter ounce ; rectified spirit (60 O. P.), five pints ; coloring, a sufficiency; cordial syrup, eleven pints. Dissolve the oil in the spirit as before, add the syrup, shake all together, and if not bright in a few hours, fine with alum and tartar.

175—CINNAMON.

Oil of cinnamon, quarter ounce ; rectified spirit (60 O. P.), five pints; cordial syrup, eleven pints ; boiling water, four pints. Color with burnt sugar. The oil and coloring matter should be well shaken with a small quantity of spirit, then added to the remainder and the whole agitated briskly. Add the boiling water to the syrup, and having mixed them let them be added to the jar containing the spirit. If necessary, fine down with alum, &c., as with the others. In making the above a considerable saving may be effected by using oil of cassia ; the true cinnamon flavor is, of course, wanting, but is so well represented by that of oil of cassia that none but the most experienced can detect the difference.

176—CAPILLAIRE.

Best lump sugar, twenty pounds ; water, ten pints ; acetic acid, strong, one drachm. Boil the sugar in the water till it is all dissolved ; add the acetic acid and allow it to remain ten or fifteen minutes on the fire ; remove and allow it to cool; then decant it ; clear into a bottle or jar.

177—LEMON.

Essential oil of lemon, three drops ; lemon juice, three pints ; lemon peel, fresh, six ounces ; refined sugar, six pounds ; rectified spirit, two pints. Add the oil to the juice, and in it boil the peel, which should be cut very small ; strain ; add to the strained liquor the sugar ; dissolve by aid of gentle heat, and when cool, mix in the spirit by brisk agitation.

178—GINGER.

Bruise half a pound of the best new Jamaica ginger in an iron mortar, and put it into a bottle containing one pint of spirit of wine (60 O. P.), and one pint of water, allow it to macerate for ten or twelve days, shaking it well up each morning. After the twelfth day transfer it to a funnel containing a paper filter ; when all the liquid has run through, pass two pints of sherry over it, and lastly, one pint of boiling water. This will yield rather better than half a gallon of liquid. When all are mixed, dissolve in this one ounce of burnt sugar, and having added twelve pints of syrup, shake the whole well up, and fine with alum, &c.

179—GINGER GIN.

Take of best Jamaica ginger, bruised small, half a

pound; boil it in one gallon of water, and strain through fine muslin. In this dissolve ten pounds of refined sugar by means of a gentle heat. Over the bruised ginger which remains in the muslin strainer pass one gallon unmixed gin (O. P.), mix this and the syrup of ginger together, add finings, and set aside to clear.

180—GINGER BRANDY.

This may be made by following the same directions as given for ginger gin, or the following will be found more economical though taking a longer time to prepare. Steep half a pound of well bruised Jamaica ginger in one gallon of strong brandy for fourteen days, shaking it up repeatedly. Let this be strained through muslin. Throw the ginger from the muslin into a gallon of boiling water and allow it to simmer over a low fire for twenty minutes, and strain. To this add ten pounds of refined sugar.

181—PEPPERMINT.

Mitcham oil of peppermint, one drachm; rectified spirit (60 O. P.), three pints; cordial syrup, thirteen pints. Proceed as in the foregoing

182—LOVAGE.

Essential oil of nutmegs, one drachm; oil of cinnamon, one drachm; oil of carraway, forty drops; rectified spirit (60 O. P.), three pints; cordial syrup, thirteen pints; spirit coloring, two ounces. Dissolve all the oils together in the spirit; next add the coloring matter; and lastly, mix in the syrup a quart at a time, shaking well between each addition. For fining, use alum and tartar in the usual way.

183.—RASPBERRY.

Essence of raspberry, eight ounces; spirit of wine (53 O. P.) two and a half pints; cordial syrup, thirteen pints; tincture of cudbear, strong, two ounces. Let all these be shaken well up together in a jar, using no finings, for if the materials are genuine, the cordial will be bright and ready for use the day it is mixed.

184—STRAWBERRY.

Essence of strawberry, six ounces; rectified spirit (60 O. P.), three pints; tincture of cudbear, two ounces; cordial syrup, thirteen pints. Proceed as with raspberry

185—NOYEAU.

Bitter oil of almonds, one drachm; oil of cinnamon, twenty drops; rectified spirit, three pints; cordial syrup, thirteen pints; tincture of cudbear, enough to give a slight pink tinge. Dissolve the oil as usual, add the syrup, and if necessary fine with alum, &c.

186—USQUEBAUGH.

Oil of aniseed, one drachm; oil of cloves, one drachm; essential oil of nutmegs, one drachm; oil of cinnamon, twenty drops; oil of juniper, thirty drops. Mix all the oils together, shaking well occasionally for a day or so; then dissolve them in rectified spirit (60 O. P.), one pint; colored with burnt sugar, one ounce; and add of each, syrup and boiling water, twelve pints. Mix all together thoroughly and fine with alum, &c.

187—CORDIAL SYRUP.

Refined lump sugar, thirty pounds; boiling water, three gallons. Dissolve the sugar in the water, and strain through flannel.

188—RUM SHRUB.

Bitter orange juice, half gallon; refined sugar, eight pounds; rum, reduced to 40 U. P., one and a half gallons. Dissolve the sugar in the juice by aid of a gentle heat, mix this and the rum together; shake well up and set aside to clear; if not bright in a fortnight fine down with isinglass.

LIQUEURS.

189—ANISETEE.

Powdered aniseed, nine ounces; powdered cummin seed, one ounce; powdered orris root, one ounce; lemon peel, three ounces; spirits (30 U. P.), two gallons; capillaire, three pints. Macerate the powders and peel in the spirits for about a month, then filter and add the capillaire.

190—AQUA BIANCA.

Essence of lemon, quarter ounce; essence of citron, quarter ounce; essence of amber, quarter ounce; essence of peppermint, quarter ounce; essence of bergamot, quarter ounce; essence of rose, quarter ounce; proof of spirit, two gallons; capillaire, five pints. Mix all together; shake frequently, and in one month filter through flannel.

191—CORDIALE DE CALADON.

Lemon peel, cut small, half a pound; fennel seed, in coarse powder, half an ounce; cardamoms, quarter ounce; aniseed, one drachm; cloves, one drachm; proof spirit, two gallons; capillaire, four pints. Macerate the peel and the powders in the spirit for fourteen days; then press and filter, and add the capillaire.

192—CITRON.

Lemon peel, twelve ounces; essence of saffron, one ounce; proof spirit, two gallons; capillaire, half gallon.

Macerate the peel in the spirit for fourteen days, then add the essence of saffron and capillaire.

193—CITRIONETTE

Proof spirit, two gallons; orange flower water, quarter gallon; syrup, half gallon; lemon peel, ten ounces; essence of saffron, one and a half ounces; essence of amber, quarter ounce; essence of orange, quarter ounce; essence of bergamot, one drachm. Mix altogether, and in one month press and filter. This is greatly improved by age.

194—CITRONELLE.

Plain spirit (14 U. P.), two gallons; cloves, one drachm; nutmegs, one drachm; syrup, two pints; lemon peel. ten ounces; essence of saffron, two ounces. Macerate the solids in the spirit for one month; press, filter, and add the essence of saffron and syrup.

195—CHRISTOPHELET.

Powdered orris root, one ounce; powdered aniseed, one ounce; powdered cinnamon, half an ounce; powdered coriander, half an ounce; powdered cardamoms, quarter ounce; powdered galenga, quarter ounce; sage, the fresh herb, half an ounce; saffron, one ounce; wine, Burgundy or Bordeaux, half gallon; rectified spirit (11 O. P), one and a half gallons; capillaire, half gallon. Macerate all the solids in the spirits for about one month; then press and filter, and add the wine and capillaire.

196—CURACAO.

Orange peel, cut small, six ounces; cinnamon, one drachm; mace, bruised, half drachm; saffron, one drachm; spirit of wine (14 U. P.), one and a quarter gallons; capillaire, two pints. Macerate all together; in about twenty-one days draw off the liquor through a strainer, and press the residue so as to recover any of the liquor it may have retained; mix both liquors, and filter through flannel.

197—EAU D'ABSINTHE.

Lemon peel, cut small, half pound; wormwood, cut small, one pound; rectified spirit (11 O. P.), one and a half gallons; capillaire, half gallon. Macerate the wormwood and the peel in the spirit for about a month; then press and filter, and add the capillaire. Some color this green.

198—EAU D'ABSINTHE (French).

Wormwood, thirty-three ounces; refined sugar, twenty-four ounces; juniper berries, four ounces; angelica root, quarter ounce; cinnamon bark, one ounce; orange flower water, four ounces; spirit of wine (11 U. P.), two and a half gallons. Bruise the sugar, berries, wormwood, &c., in an iron mortar or other convenient utensil and place them in a wide mouthed jar, then add the orange water and spirit. Stir them well up every day for a month, then press and filter.

199—EAU CELESTE.

Essence of cloves, two drachms; essence of fennel, one drachm; essence of lemon, one ounce; essence of aniseed, one drachm; essence of cummin, one drachm; essence of cinnamon, two drachms; essence of violet flowers, half an ounce; proof spirit, two gallons; capillaire, half gallon. Mix all the essences together and add them to the spirits; then add them to the capillaire. This may be used at once, but it improves greatly by keeping.

200—EAU DE CORDIALE.

Lemon peel, cut small, twenty ounces; cinnamon bark, bruised, four ounces; balm, the fresh herb, two ounces; powdered coriander seed, two ounces; powdered aniseed, two ounces; powdered mace, one ounce; powdered nutmegs, one ounce; rectified spirit (60 O. P.), two and a half gallons; distilled or rain water, one and three-quarter gallons; capillaire, one gallon. Macerate the solids for ten days in the spirits, and decant as much liquor as can be got off clear. To the marc add the water and capillaire; stir well up and set aside for fourteen days; then press, filter, and add the liquor first withdrawn. Another method, and we think a better one, is to mix all the ingredients together and stir them well up every other morning for about a month, and then to press and filter.

201—EAU D'AMIS.

Figs, dates and raisins, of each, four ounces; essence of saffron, one ounce; essence of bergamote, six drops; essence of citron, ten drops; proof spirit, one and a half gallons; brown sugar, ten pounds; distilled water, six pints. Beat up the figs, dates, &c., with a part of the sugar until they form a smooth paste; place this in a wide mouthed jar, and having previously mixed together the liquids, add a quart at a time, stirring well between each addition; lastly, add the balance of the sugar, and in one month press and filter.

202--EAU DE BATAVE (Dutch Water).

Juniper berries, bruised, three ounces; lemon peel, cut small, two ounces; powdered cinnamon, six drachms; powdered nutmegs, ninety grains; essence of cloves, one ounce; proof spirit, two gallons; capillaire, half gallon. Macerate the solids in the spirit for a month, shaking well every morning; then add the essence of cloves and capillaire, and in a day or two press and filter.

203—EAU DE CLARET.

Carraway, coriander, fennel, daucus creticus, dill and aniseed, of each, three ounces; refined lump sugar, three pounds; proof spirit, one and a half gallons. Macerate for a month, then filter.

204—EAU DE DIDON.

Lemon peel, cut small, six ounces ; figs, bruised, six ounces ; balm, three ounces ; powdered grains of paradise, one ounce ; camomile flowers, two ounces ; powdered cinnamon, half an ounce ; powdered aniseed, half an ounce ; powdered nutmegs, quarter of an ounce ; essence of violet flowers, two ounces ; proof spirit, two gallons ; capillaire, half a gallon. Let all the above be mixed thoroughly together ; shake up every day for a fortnight, then press and filter.

205—EAU D'OR.

Orange peel, six ounces ; lemon peel, three ounces; juniper berries, half an ounce ; rosemary leaves, half an ounce ; powdered cinnamon, half an ounce ; powdered aniseed, half an ounce ; powdered orris root, quarter of an ounce ; nutmegs, quarter of an ounce ; cloves, one drachm ; cardamoms, one drachm ; proof spirit, two gallons; capillaire, half a gallon ; gold foil a few leaves.

206—EAU D'OR—(German).

Lemon peel, four ounces; cinnamon, three drachms ; Mace, one drachm ; coriander, one drachm ; proof spirit, two gallons ; capillaire, half gallon ; gold foil, a few leaves.

207—EAU D'ARGENT (German).

Lemon peel, two ounces ; balm, one ounce ; cinnamon, quarter of an ounce ; cloves, half an ounce ; angelica seed, one and a half drachms ; aniseed, one and a half drachms ; orris root, one and a half drachms ; proof spirit, two gallons ; capillaire, half a gallon.   Silver foil, a few leaves.

208—EAU D'ARGENT

Lily flowers, three ounces ; bitter almonds, two ounces ; powdered cinnamon, one ounce ; powdered peppermint, half an ounce ; powdered nutmegs, half an ounce ; powdered aniseed, half an ounce; powdered angelica, quarter of an ounce; cloves, one drachm; proof spirit, two gallons; capillaire, half gallon; silver foil, a few leaves.

209—EAU DES PRINCESSES.

No. 1.—Balm, figs, orange peel, cassia, lavender flowers, of each, one ounce; camomile flowers, bitter almonds, rosemary leaves, of each, one drachm; powdered cloves, forty grains; essence of amber, twelve drops; proof spirit, two gallons; capillaire, half gallon; gold foil, a few leaves.

No. 2.—Proof spirit, two gallons; lavender flowers, four ounces; cinnamon, aniseed and lemon peel, each, one ounce; camomile flowers, half an ounce; essence of lemon, one drachm; essence of amber, one drachm; capillaire, five pints.

In making any of the last six compounds, macerate the solids for twenty-one days in the spirit; then press and filter; add one half of the capillaire, and fill into small clear glass bottles, leaving room in each. Into a wide mouthed bottle put the rest of the capillaire and the silver or gold foil, and with an egg switch beat up till the foil is broken into grains not larger than a pin head. With this fill up the bottles.

210—EAU DE GENIEVRE.

Fresh juniper berries, half a pound; brown sugar, six pounds; spirit (30 U. P.), two gallons. Bruise the berries with a portion of the sugar; then add all together; shake every morning for a month; then press and filter.

211—EAU DE NAP (Napoleon.)

Orange flower water, two pints; peppermint water, one pint; rose water, two pints; powdered nutmegs, half ounce; powdered cinnamon, six drachms; powdered cloves, six drachms; essence vanilla, thirty drops; essence violet flowers, quarter ounce; lemon peel, cut small, two and a half ounces; jasmin flowers, fresh, two ounces; capillaire, half gallon; rectified spirit (60 O. P.), quarter gallon. Mix all together, and after shaking the mixture well up every day for a month, filter.

212—EAU DE NOBLES.

Rose leaves, four ounces; orange peel, cut small, three ounces; powdered cinnamon, half an ounce; powdered nutmegs, one drachm; powdered cloves, two drachms; proof spirit, two gallons; capillaire, five pints. Macerate all the ingredients together for one month, then press and filter. Color with essence of cochineal, and add twenty drops of essence of vanilla.

213—EAU NUPTIALE.

Parsley seed, bruised, one and a half ounces; carrot seed, one and a quarter ounces; aniseed, half ounce; orris root, half ounce; saffron, three drachms; powdered mace, three drachms; rectified spirit (11 O. P.), two gallons; rose water, quarter gallon; capillaire, half gallon. Macerate for one month, shaking frequently, then filter.

214—EAU DE POLOGNE.

Galengal, marjoram, rosemary, cloves, cassia, mint, aniseed, fennel, of each, quarter ounce; raisins, quarter pound; rectified spirit (60 O. P.), one gallon; rose water, one gallon; capillaire, three pints. Mix all together; shake every morning for a month; then filter.

215—EAU DE TEMPLIERS.

Orange peel, cut small, 2 ounces; rosemary leaves, half an ounce; laurel berries, half ounce; powdered cinnamon, quarter ounce; powdered aniseed, quarter ounce; essence of vanilla, thirty drops; essence of lemon, twenty drops; rose water, one pint; orange flower water, one pint; rectified spirits (60 O. P.), five pints; capillaire, two pints; violet flowers, one ounce. Proceed as for Eau de Pologne.

216—EAU DE VIE DE DANTZIC.

Lemon peel, cut small, four ounces; orange flowers, four ounces; bitter almonds, bruised, four ounces; rose leaves, eight ounces; gum mastic, half an ounce; rectified spirits (11 O. P.), two gallons; capillaire, half gallon. Macerate for five or six weeks, shaking the mixture each second day, then filter.

217—EAU DE VIE DE DANTZIC.

Celery seed, bruised, one ounce; carraway seed, bruised, one ounce; aniseed, bruised, one ounce; orange peel, cut small, one ounce; proof spirit, one and a half gallons; capillaire, half gallon. Proceed as above.

218—ESCUBAC.

Raisins and dates, each, four ounces; juniper berries, four ounces; saffron, one ounce; proof spirit, one and a quarter gallons. Beat the fruit with its pips and kernels into a smooth paste; mix it and the saffron with the spirit and macerate for fourteen days; press, and add: essence of coriander, one ounce; essence of mace, one ounce; essence of cloves, one ounce; essence of aniseed, one ounce; essence of cinnamon, two ounces; capillaire, one gallon. Shake well up every morning for a month, then filter.

219—ESCUBAC

Raisins and dates, each, four ounces; saffron, two ounces; powdered cinnamon, eighty grains; powdered aniseed, seventy grains; powdered coriander, eighty grains; proof spirit, two gallons; capillaire, half gallon. Beat up all the solids with a little capillaire until a smooth paste is obtained, mix this and the spirit together and shake up every morning for a month, then add the capillaire and filter.

220—JASMIN.

Proof spirit, ten pints; capillaire, five pints; essence of jasmin, enough to flavor; mix.

221—LIQUEUR DE MENTHE.

Peppermint leaves, one pound; powdered aniseed, one ounce; capillaire, half gallon; proof spirit, two gallons. Macerate for one month, then press and filter.

222—LIQUEUR D'ORANGE.

Orange peel, fresh, eight ounces; orange flower water, quarter gallon; capillaire, half gallon; proof spirit, one and three-quarter gallons. Proceed as above.

223—LIQUEUR DE ROSE.

Red rose leaves, one pound; cinnamon bark, six drachms; fennel seeds, two drachms; capillaire, half gallon; spirit (11 U. P.), two and a quarter gallons. Proceed as for liqueur d'orange.

224—LUFT WASSER.

Cinnamon bark, cummin seeds, sweet fennel, lavender flowers, camomile flowers, powdered orris root, and rosemary leaves, of each, one ounce; sassafras and sage, of each, quarter ounce; figs, eight ounces; water, seven pints; capillaire, half gallon; rectified spirits (63 O. P), one and a quarter gallons. Macerate the leaves, seeds, &c., in the spirits for twenty-one days, shaking frequently; then drain off the liquor into a bottle. Over the residue from which the spirit has been withdrawn pour the water, shake up well every morning for other seven days, then press and filter. Now mix together the two liquors and the capillaire, and if not bright filter through a little magnesia.

225—MARACHINO.

Black cherries, two pounds; raspberries, three pounds; orange flowers, one pound; proof spirit, two gallons; capillaire, three-quarter gallon. Break the fruit down with the hand in a little of the spirits; remove the cherry stones, and beat them up in a mortar; then mix all the ingredients together and macerate for a month. Decant the clear liquor; press out that which remains in the fruit, and having added both together, filter.

226—MARACHINO.

Finest dried prunes, three pounds; raspberries, two pounds; cherry leaves, eight ounces; powdered orris root, one ounce; essence of almonds, one drachm; proof spirits, two and a half gallons; capillaire, half gallon. Proceed as above.

227—MONPON.

Essence of peppermint, cloves, aniseed, cinnamon, and vanilla, of each, thirty drops; rose, elder flower and distilled water, of each, two pints; capillaire, three-quarter gallon; rectified spirit (60 O. P.), one and three-quarter gallons. Mix all the essences together, and add them to the spirits. Mix the waters together and add them to the capillaire; gradually add the latter mixtures to the former, shaking up well during the operation. If in a week or two it should not be bright enough for use, filter it through a paper filter containing three ounces or so of carbonate of magnesia.

228—NOYEAU.

No. 1.—Peach, apricot, and plum kernels, of each, two and a half ounces; brown sugar, two pounds; orange flower water, half a pint; spirit (16 U. P.), one gallon. Beat the kernels into a smooth paste, adding a little highly rectified spirits during the process; mix all together, and shake up every morning for a month, then filter.

No. 2.—Apricot and peach kernels, of each, four ounces; capillaire, two pints; proof spirit, one gallon. Proceed as above.

229—PARFAIT AMOUR.

No. 1.—Orange peel, cut small, quarter ounce; powdered cloves, quarter ounce; brown sugar, ten pounds; distilled water, one gallon; proof spirit, two gallons. Dissolve the sugar in the water by the aid of a gentle heat; macerate the peel and cloves in two pints of the spirit for three or four weeks, then filter and add all the liquids together.

No. 2.—Proof spirit, two gallons; capillaire, half gallon; lemon peel, cut small, eight ounces; cinnamon bark, one and a half ounces; orange flowers, one ounce; rosemary leaves, half ounce; powdered cloves, half ounce; powdered cardamoms, half ounce; powdered mace, quarter ounce; saffron, one ounce. Macerate the solids in one gallon of the spirit for a month, shaking the mixture frequently; then filter and add all the liquids together.

230—PERSICOT.

Bitter almonds, six ounces; cinnamon bark, one-eighth of an ounce; essence of cochineal, quarter ounce; proof spirit, one and a half gallons; capillaire, two pints. Macerate ten days; then filter. This is sometimes made without the cinnamon or the essence of cochineal.

231—PERSICOT (Dutch).

Bitter almonds, bruised, one pound; cinnamon bark, half ounce; lemon peel, cut small, two ounces; powdered cloves, one-eighth of an ounce; powdered nutmegs; one-eighth of an ounce; saffron, sixty grains; proof spirit, two and three-quarter gallons; capillaire, three-quarters of a gallon. Macerate three weeks, then press and filter.

232—ROSOLIS.

Petals of red roses, four ounces; orange flowers, two ounces; extract of jasmin, one ounce; cloves, whole, forty grains; cinnamon bark, sixty grains; rectified spirit (60 O. P.), three-quarter gallon; water, half gallon; capillaire, one pint.

233—ROSOLIS (French).

Powdered nutmegs, half ounce; cinnamon, one ounce; powdered orris root, half ounce; powdered cardamoms, half ounce; rose water, four pints; rectified spirit (60 O. P), five pints; capillaire, two pints.

234—ROSOLIS (Dutch).

Powdered angelica, one drachm; powdered aniseed, one drachm; powdered cardamoms, one drachm; powdered cloves, one drachm; powdered cinnamon, half ounce; lemon peel, one and a half ounces; rectified spirit (60 O. P.), five pints; water, one pint; capillaire, two pints.

235—ROSOLIS (De Turin).

Jessamine flowers, three ounces; orange flowers, four ounces; rose buds, four ounces; raisins, four ounces; powdered cinnamon, three drachms; powdered cloves, two drachms; rectified spirit (60 O. P.), five pints; water, four pints; capillaire, two pints. The simplest and best plan to adopt in making these four liqueurs is to mix the spirit with the water, and macerate all the solids in the mixture for about twenty-one days, stirring them up with a glass rod every morning; then decant the liquid and press the residue dry; mix what has been decanted and that which has been pressed out, and filter through paper. Lastly, add the capillaire. Color the two first rose-pink, the last scarlet.

236—USQUEBAUGH.

Powdered cinnamon, three ounces; lavender flowers, free

from stalk, one ounce ; powdered cloves, half ounce ; powdered aniseed, half ounce ; powdered nutmegs, half ounce ;
saffron, half ounce ; whole cardamoms, quarter ounce ;
proof spirit, one gallon ; capillaire, half gallon. Steep the
solids in the spirit fourteen days ; press and filter, then add
the capillaire.

237—VESPETRO.

Powdered fennel seeds, half ounce ; powdered coriander
seeds, half ounce ; powdered carraway seeds, half ounce ;
powdered angelica seeds, half ounce ; essence of orange, half
ounce ; essence of cochineal, quarter ounce ; brown sugar,
five pounds ; spirits (30 U. P.), one and a half gallons.
Macerate for a month, then decant or filter.

238—VESPETRO (French).

One lemon and one orange, sliced ; coriander seeds,
whole, half ounce ; angelica seeds, bruised, half ounce ; fennel seeds, one-eighth of an ounce ; aniseed, one-eighth of an
ounce ; proof spirit, one and a quarter gallons ; capillaire, one
pint.   Proceed as above.

BITTERS.

The trifling cost and little trouble attached to the manufacture of bitters, induces us to give a greater variety of
receipts for their production, than can probably be found in
any other collection. We take this step knowing the very
great convenience they will afford the proprietor, not only
in regulating his stock to the tastes and requirements of
his customers, but also in giving him a power of graduating
the strength of the article he may desire. This he can do

readily by simply using a higher or lower proof of spirit, at the outset.

239—ABSINTHE OR WORMWOOD BITTERS.

Oil of lemon, oil of carraway, and oil of absinthe, of each, two drops; extract of liquorice, two ounces; extract of camomile, half ounce; rectified spirit, (60 O. P.) three pints; syrup, three pints; water, enough to make two gallons. Dissolve the oils in the spirit, and the extracts in water, add both together at once, shake violently for some minutes; next add the syrup and the remainder of the water, and again shake well up. Let it stand aside some days, the longer the better, then filter through paper.

240—ANGUSTURA BITTERS.

Angustura bark, four ounces; camomile flowers, one ounce; cardamom seeds, quarter ounce; cinnamon bark, qnarter ounce; orange peel, one ounce; raisins, one pound; proof spirits, two and a half gallons. Macerate for a month, then press and filter.

241—BRANDY BITTERS.

Gentian root, four pounds; orange peel, four pounds; cardamom seeds, two pounds; cinnamon bark, one pound; cochineal, quarter pound; chireta, two pounds. Bruise all these together to the size of barley corns; then add two gallons of brandy. Macerate for about a month, then press out all the liquid; to the residue add one gallon more brandy (some use plain spirit), and after having allowed it to stand one day, press as before; add the two liquids and filter, when it will be ready for use.

242—DUTCH BITTERS.

Wormwood, two ounces; camomile flowers, one ounce; gentian root, one ounce; orange peel, two ounces; powdered cloves, one-eighth of an ounce; carraway seeds, quar-

ter ounce ; capillaire, half gallon ; proof spirit, two gallons.
Macerate for a month, then press and filter.

243—ORANGE BITTERS.

Take freshly dried orange peel, one pound ; coriander
seeds, one ounce ; carraway seeds, one drachm ; cardamom
seeds, one drachm ; rectified spirits (60 O. P.), five pints ;
burnt sugar, two ounces ; syrup, six pints ; water, sufficient
to make up to two gallons. Steep the seeds and peel in the
spirit for fourteen or twenty days, when it must be drained off
and replaced by water ; which after two days drain off and
replace by a second quantity of water. Let the three tinc-
tures thus obtained be mixed together, and first the coloring
and then the syrup be added. This, if allowed to remain a
short time undisturbed, will become bright ; or if wanted for
immediate use, may be filtered through fine linen.

244—" PICK-ME-UP " BITTERS.

Angustura bark, one ounce ; orange peel, one ounce ;
lemon peel, one ounce ; chiretta, half ounce ; camomile
flowers, half ounce ; cardamom seeds, quarter ounce ; cinnamon bark, quarter ounce ; carraway seeds, quarter ounce ;
raisins, four pounds ; spirits (11 U. P.), one and a half gallons. Macerate for a month, then press and filter.

245—QUININE BITTERS.

Sulphate of quinine, one hundred and sixty grains ; orange
peel, cut small, one pound ; cape wine, two gallons ; proof
spirit, one pint. Dissolve the quinine in the spirit by aid
of a gentle heat, and pour it over the orange peel. After it
has been allowed to remain undisturbed in a close vessel
for two days, add the wine, and stir up well every day for
a fortnight, then press and filter.

246—QUININE WINE.

Sulphate of quinine, one ounce ; citric acid, one and a

half ounce; orange wine, three gallons. Dissolve first the acid, and then the quinine, in the wine; allow the solution to remain for seven days in a close vessel, shaking occasionally; then filter. A small wine glass of this forms an excellent stomachic.

POPULAR AERATED WATERS.

247—LEMONADE.

This is generally prepared by putting into each bottle one ounce of syrup of lemons, and then filling them up with aërated water from the machine.

248—RASPBERRYADE.

This is made in the same way as the above, merely substituting the syrup of raspberry for that of lemon. Many attempts have been made to impart to this preparation a red color that will be permanent, but no vegetable red will withstand the action of acids, and all mineral colorings are more or less dangerous.

249—ORANGEADE.

In making this, add to each bottle one ounce of syrup of orange, and proceed as for lemonade.

250—AERATED GINGERBEER.

A very great variety of methods are adopted in making this, but owing to the great difficulty of getting a perfectly bright article—one entirely free from milkiness—it will be safer for the beginner to follow the old and simple plan of drawing from the machine plain aërated water into bottles, in each of which one ounce of syrup of ginger has been placed. Receipts for this and other syrups have been given in another part of this work.

251—SPARKLING NECTAR.

This is simply highly aërated water drawn from the machine into bottles containing syrup of nectar.

252—SPARKLING CIDER.

This, and a number of similar named beverages (such as champagne cider, &c.,) are merely aërated water flavored by the addition of pineapple, jargonelle, or other syrup.

CONCENTRATED FRUIT SYRUPS

The strength of all the following syrups has been calculated solely with a view to the convenience of hotel keepers, publicans, &c. They being very different from articles sold under similar names, we advise each party to prepare them for themselves : and this can be done with little or no trouble, by making two or three gallons of the simple syrup as a stock, from which a pint or two can be taken at any time, and flavored with any of the fruit essences as required. In summer, one ounce added to a bottle of aërated water or soda water, will produce a glass of orangeade, lemonade, nectar, or other such beverage as may be required, thus obviating the necessity of keeping a stock of each of these in bottle. In winter they may be used instead of sugar for sweetening hot drinks, such as gin, rum, &c., to which they impart the agreeable flavor of the fruit whose name they bear. They are also used as a base for the various acidulated summer beverages, receipts for preparing which we have given further on.

· 253—SIMPLE SYRUP.

Refined sugar, seven pounds ; distilled water, three pints. Dissolve the sugar in the water over a gentle fire.

254—CLOVE SYRUP.

Quintessence of cloves, thirty drops; simple syrup, one pound. Mix by shaking well up together in a bottle.

255—RASPBERRY SYRUP.

Essence of raspberries, two drachms; simple syrup, one pint. Mix.

256—STRAWBERRY SYRUP.

Essence of strawberries, one drachm ; simple syrup, one pound. Mix.

257—PINEAPPLE SYRUP.

Essence of pineapple, twenty drops; simple syrup, one pound. Mix.

258—JARGONELLE SYRUP.

Essence of jargonelle pears, twenty drops ; simple syrup, one pound. Mix.

259—LEMON SYRUP.

Tincture of lemon peel, two ounces ; simple syrup, one pound. Mix.

260—ORANGE SYRUP.

Tincture of orange peel, two ounces ; simple syrup, one pound. Mix.

261—SYRUP OF NECTAR.

Essence of nectar, thirty drops; simple syrup, one pound. Mix.

262—SYRUP OF GINGER.

Essence of ginger, one ounce; simple syrup, one pound. Mix.

263—SYRUP OF PEACH KERNEL.

Eessence of peach kernel, thirty drops; simple syrup, one pound.   Mix.

Sage, mint, ratafia, noyeau, vanilla, or any other syrup may be made in like manner with the above; that necessary strength being arrived at by adding the essence gradually to the simple syrup, till the desired flavor is obtained.

Acidulated Summer Beverages.

One or two ounces (a small wine glass full) of any of the following acidulated syrups, added to a tumbler full of iced or spring water forms a most delicious and refreshing draught in warm weather, or when the palate has become vitiated and the stomach heated by the too frequent use of alcoholics.

264—ACIDULATED LEMONADE.

Syrup of lemons, one pint; acidifying solution, one ounce.   Mix.

265—RASPBERRY VINEGAR.

Acidifying solution, one ounce; raspberry syrup, one pint.   Mix.

266—STRAWBERRY VINEGAR.

Acidifying solution, one ounce; strawberry syrup, one pint. Mix.

267—ACCIDULATED ORANGEADE.

Syrup of orange, one pint; acidifying solution, one ounce. Mix. Proceed in like manner with any of the other syrups.

268—ACIDIFYING SOLUTION.

Powdered citric acid, one pound; distilled water, one pint. Dissolve the acid in the water by aid of a gentle heat, and filter while hot, through fine muslin.

MISCELLANEOUS WINES.

269—ARTIFICIAL CHAMPAGNE.

Boil together over a slow fire fourteen pounds of each, best lump and moist sugar, in fifteen gallons of distilled or rain water; skim this, and while yet warm pour into a cask, to which add two hundred and fifty grains of citric acid dissolved in half a pint of water and a sufficient quantity of yeast. Having placed the cask in a moderately cool situation, leave it to ferment. Now add, good well boiled sherry, not too dry, one gallon; genuine French brandy, one gallon; essence of strawberry juice, half gallon; tincture of cochineal, one pint; previously mixed together and filtered.

Printed in Great Britain
by Amazon